WHEN A MUSTARD SEED GETS HEAVY

Poetic Expressions Of Life, Lessons, And Love

Ricky Lamon Davis

Copyright © 2025 by Ricky Lamon Davis
Los Angeles California
All rights reserved.
Printed and Bound in the United States of America

Published And Distributed By
True Capacity Publishing House
Los Angeles, California
Email: rickylamondavis@gmail.com

Packaging/Consulting
Professional Publishing House
1425 W. Manchester Ave. Ste B
Los Angeles, California 90047
323-750-3592
Email: professionalpublishinghouse@yahoo.com
www.Professionalpublishinghouse.com

Cover Design by Daryl's Designs
First printing April 2025
ISBN: 979-8-218-63633-3
10 9 8 7 6 5 4 3 2 1

No part of this book may be reproduced, stored in a retrieval system or transmitted in any form or by any means without the prior written permission of the publisher—except by a reviewer who may quote brief passages in a review to be printed in a newspaper, magazine or journal. For inquiries contact the publisher: rickylamondavis@gmail.com.

In Memory of
Earnestine Pierre (1932-2022)

My loving grandmother always told me, "Don't worry about what people say about you; worry when no one is saying anything at all."

Her wisdom stemmed from countless conversations during my childhood about classmates and neighborhood bullies who picked on me for not participating in juvenile behavior. I struggled with feeling accepted by my peers.

It wasn't until I became an adult that my grandmother's words changed my perspective, giving me the confidence to walk boldly with better self-esteem and to stop focusing on others' perceptions of me. Whether I do good or bad, people will always have something to say.

That's why I focus on God's assignment for my life and how He chooses to use me as a vessel.

Lastly, my loving grandmother stood by the phrase, "Your older days will be your better days." I'm a living witness to the peace that resonates in my heart.

My grandmother was saved and loved Jesus! I know she is in the presence of the Lord, and I miss her dearly. However, her words will continue to echo in my mind as a reminder to never put faith and trust in man, but only in God.

Thank you, Grandma, and I look forward to seeing you again.

Dedicated to...

Candace April Amie, a woman of resilience and strength who endured the loss of her husband and father and survived a serious car accident—all within a short period of time.

With support from me and others, Candace made the courageous decision to begin therapy, facing her grief, pain, anger, resentment, and guilt head-on.

Despite the many moments when giving up felt easier, she committed herself to healing and learning to trust God more fully.

Through it all, Candace's heart and contagious personality continue to uplift and encourage me, her family, friends, co-workers, and everyone blessed to cross her path.

I'm humbled to write this book as a source of encouragement for anyone going through something they didn't ask for or see coming. Just know—whatever doesn't break you completely will make you stronger.

Thank you, Candace, for allowing God to use you in such a comforting and powerful way, and for inspiring me to finish this book. You continue to show how faith grows through prayer, perseverance, and surrender.

TABLE OF CONTENTS

Preface ix

Section 1: Life

Faith Check 3
Man Cry 5
Why Me 6
Should Time Wait 8
Circles 10
Hate the Game 12
Selfishly Impatient 14
Pullout Game 16
Dog Ears 18
War Within 20

Section 2: Lessons

Waiting May Endure 23
NO Power 24
Fake Grass 26
Break My Fall 28
Love My Hate 29
Ignorantly Blind 31
Artificiality 33
Tailor Made 34
Blood Water 36

Grand of Things 38

Section 3: Love

LuvFriend 43
Still Love 45
Matching Luggage 47
Daddy Man 49
Couch Talk 51
Fluent Love 53
I Will Find You 55
Music Me 57
Quantum Covenant 59
Love Is 61

About the Author 63

Preface

I wrote this book to uplift anyone needing encouragement and inspiration right now. I know it's frustrating when things continue to happen, and we ask ourselves, "Why me?" However, we must stay hopeful that things will get better. The three sections of this book—LIFE, LESSONS, and LOVE—are a reflection of the personal experiences we encounter in our everyday lives.

Like you, I am regularly tested and wonder when this will end. How much do I have to suffer? Is life supposed to be this hard? When will my breakthrough come? Hopefully, this book will answer these questions and lead you in the direction of restoration, rebuilding, and renewal in your life.

I know you've been disappointed and hurt in past or present relationships. Like me, maybe you've experienced resentment, bitterness, and trust issues. With the help of therapy, I've learned how to manage my emotions and feelings, how to forgive others, and how to be accountable for my actions. Through countless therapy sessions, I've discovered that it's impossible to love and care for anyone unconditionally until you start with self. Dealing with emotional scars and wounds from childhood to adulthood plays a significant role in how we view relationships. I'm grateful I invested in my mental health so I can be more relational with my kids, family, friends, and that special someone.

Lastly, my inspiration for writing this book was influenced by those who poured into my life in significant ways. When I really needed direction, God sent individuals to encourage and mentor me. The late Dr. Johnny V. Baylor was not only a mentor but also my pastor and spiritual father for almost 20 years. Dr. Baylor taught me how to live in my truest capacity as a man and how to seek an understanding of everything before making emotional decisions. He once shared in a men's Bible study that, "We can't do life on any level effectively if we don't relax and have an RMA—Relaxed Mental Attitude. He also taught us, "We may not win the relationship, but we can still win the war." This source of encouragement gave me a healthier perspective on choosing my battles in relationships and doing more listening than talking. I also learned that it's not about winning or losing but giving your best effort regardless of the end results.

Bishop Terry L. Brown, my pastor and mentor, encouraged and challenged me to write this book. He profoundly illustrated the definition of God's love in the simplest form. He said, "Love is a minimum of emotion, a maximum of commitment, seeking the good toward the object of your concern by doing what needs to be done with a spirit of self-sacrifice, even when you don't feel like doing it." This expression of God's love was shared with Bishop Brown by his mentor and spiritual father, the late Dr. Albert Louis Patterson, Jr. These nuggets of knowledge and wisdom, along with my life experiences, helped prepare this book of poetic expressions, which I hope will give you encouragement and a dose of hope for your life.

SECTION 1

LIFE

Faith Check

Life is bigger than a box of sweets,
Life is tougher than slaughtered beef.
Life is complicated and unfair,
Life can drive you crazy without a spare.

My mind continues to tick backward,
Processing and overthinking without words.
Creating unnecessary thoughts without permission,
Like trying to drive without a transmission.

I really struggle with what I see,
I voted and prayed, how could this be?
I feel the enemy is laughing at me,
I hate fighting when there's no victory.

If faith is the substance of things hoped for,
The evidence of things not seen.
If I'm praying constantly and nothing changes,
Then what does faith really mean?

Is the power in prayer or faith?
How much patience do I need to wait?
Why did Jesus use the analogy of the mustard seed?
Do I put my trust in jobs or God's leads?

I need to prioritize my life,
Can't stop weeping throughout the night.
Joy is promised in the morning sunshine,
What should I do in the meantime?

Ricky Lamon Davis

The word reminds me to be courageous,
And that faith cultivates in stages.
Like mustard seeds growing into large trees,
The evidence of things not seen.

My trust should only be in God,
Not politicians, initiatives, or high-paying jobs.
By praying for man in all high-level positions,
Will my faith increase and petition God to listen?

Man Cry

Sippin' sorrow and swallowing pain,
Beaten, bruised and curled in disdain.
Fighting tears and feeling ashamed,
Life is truly driving me insane.

Rain can't fall fast enough,
To cleanse a heart so callus and rough.
Sitting at the bar puffing a cigar,
Meaningless thoughts traveling far.

If rivers flow so frequently
And oceans make waves distinctively,
Then streams must carry a certain path.
To keep vengeance from turning into wrath.

My mind's ticking to beat the clock,
So many headaches I need it to stop.
Eyes bloodshot about to pass out,
Body is tired, my soul cries out.

My trust is sinking, I have nothing left,
Always thinking, what could be next?
Should I fight to live or live to die?
I need comfort through the tears in my eyes.

Why Me

Too much hurt inside,
It's hard to comprehend.
Wish I can let it go,
And never revisit it again.

Nightmares follow me,
It's so hard to break free. I dodge every obstacle,
Fighting hard for tranquility.

Minding my own business,
Trusting the Lord almighty.
Staying clear of all distractions,
Creating distance from everybody.

Words can still cut and kill,
Processing thoughts and checking how I feel.
My character will not waver,
Because I'm covered by my Lord and Savior.

Jealousy can rage into a bloodbath,
No one should ever feel this wrath.
It all adds up when you do the math,
I need to be wise and choose the right path.

Bloody knuckles raised in protest,
What strategy should come next?
Will this lead to another conflict,
Or some asinine nonsense?

Section 1: Life

Why won't they just let me be,
Now you coming for my family.
With all the slurs and whispers,
Even those who have cursed me.

Friend circles get smaller as I grow,
Why they change, don't care to know.
My favor is not for public opinion,
Or how long someone stays in their feelings.

The world is growing insane,
This weighs heavy on my heart.
I often ask God this question,
When is it time to depart?

Should Time Wait

Time makes the mind wait,
Feelings cause huge debates.
Emotional outbursts are unrehearsed,
Which one will respond first?

If communication is slow, Will it impact my cerebral?
I handle time standing still,
To see if truth is unveiled.

Time is necessary for understanding,
Anxiously waiting is too demanding.
It's hard to fight a double mind,
When it keeps drifting further behind.

Time speaks truth to power.
Silence is golden and can last for hours.
Time sends messages and clues,
Which the heart may deem as untrue.

What's left in me is another song,
A place where I want to belong.
Where I'm touched, nurtured, and loved,
And covered like the angels above.

I'm tired of being shattered and broken,
Feeling like a penniless token.
Bloodshot tears racing down my heart,
Will time grace me with a new start?

Section 1: Life

Words never die, the heart sometimes lie,
Suffering makes me cry.
Life doesn't always care,
My flesh gets weak with nothing to spare.

Time waits for the Maker Himself,
God doesn't wait on anyone else.
Faith can't be bought, and trust is not taught,
Life can't depend on its inner self.

Time should be devoted to the King,
For he has never left nor forsaking me.
I grow stronger in faith, trust, and truth,
Time waits for no one, will God wait on you?

Circles

The sun shines on everyone,
From violent street charades.
Hustlers getting paid,
And fire hydrant spray where kids play.

Day one's been rocking since elementary,
Through all the scars, secrets, and fights.
We paid the ultimate price,
Now just trying to live life.

Friends drift and sometimes fold…
Some elevate, while others hate…
When someone wins, jealousy begins…
Circles change and nothing remains the same…

At some point you discover,
Who's real or working undercover?
Maturity will help you learn,
Which friends you need to discern.

Life is a canvas that brushes us by,
Painting false images that darken the sky.
Trying to understand the reasons why,
The truth is forbidden and covered in a lie.

God deliver me from pretentious people,
Who's words and actions can turn lethal.
I want to retaliate and use my fists,
Can't afford handcuffs on my wrists.

Section 1: Life

I want to age gracefully.
I want to live peacefully.
If my perception of people gets better.
Will the size of my circle really matter?

Hate the Game

Can't think without money on my mind,
Can't have cake without a strap by the gate.
Life's too short to move this weight,
I need to break myself before it's too late.

Been hated on since conception,
My heart bleeds, but I refuse a transfusion.
Betrayal is the ultimate disrespect,
A lot of dudes been shot and left bloody wet.

These fools want me to lose,
I lost everything, so what am I supposed to do?
I gets mine every single time,
Sticking to myself to avoid jail time.

Game from the past taught me very fast,
Can't trust man through a shiny glass.
Get caught slipping, see how long you last,
I ask God to forgive my past.

Imagine being sued for stealing shoes.
Imagine being detained because of your name…
Imagine at 102 degrees you still got cold feet…
Imagine being single in a love triangle…

Haters gonna hate and cycles come late,
Stress always second-guesses someone's incompetence.
When they see the light, illumination takes flight,
Breaking strongholds when the time's right.

Section 1: Life

Was told by Grandma, God rest her soul,
Don't worry about those who identify as foes.
When they spit on your name, it means you got game,
When they stop speaking, it means their ship's leaking.

Selfishly Impatient

My mind is a revolving door…
My heart is anxious to the core…
When sitting still I get bored…
I have what I need, but I want more…

Why are you taking so long,
You just don't get me.
You say I cleave and leave,
Impossible to please and sometimes a tease.

I'm tired of you saying not right now,
You keep this up, then I'm out.
Can't keep waiting, this ain't right,
Are you taking me to dinner tonight?

Can't be there for me, I'm cool on you,
My time is valuable, I got things to do.
I've turned down many, entertained a few,
If you waste my time, I will replace you.

Why you always looking at your schedule,
I want to travel and turn it up a level.
Why can't you be spontaneous, never mind.
I don't want to argue, let's finish this another time.

Yes, you buy me expensive things,
Purses, necklaces, and diamond rings.
You always there when I need you,
You always question if this love is true.

Section 1: Life

I really do appreciate you,
I don't just think about myself.
I hate when you always kick it with your brother,
I don't like how close you are with your mother.

You say I'm impatient,
And life don't revolve around me.
What about my biological clock, this is crazy,
Can we just get married and have a baby?

You know it's a shortage of good men,
You say I act just like my friends.
I'm tired of waiting on you,
Either make a decision or I'm through.

If I leave, what would you say…
If I give an ultimatum, will you stay…
Why can't you fight for me every day…
Why you call me selfish and turn the other way..

Pullout Game

It's hard staying on track,
With puddles underneath my back.
Do I reposition and stabilize this position,
Or complete this mission, Pullout Game.

Fastly moving you can't see me coming,
Scrambling, gambling, motionless all of sudden.
Let me slow down before the overflow,
Forget how I feel it's all the same, Pullout Game.

Mind over matter pressure in my bladder,
Fighting this feeling, eyes stuck to the ceiling.
Better or worse, who's letting go first,
Please don't scream my name, Pullout Game.

Clock ticks a quarter past nine,
So many things going through my mind.
Trying to make the best of this time,
Slow jams, red wine, damn she fine, Pullout Game.

Bodies undressed in this game of chess,
Crazy sweat dripping down my chest.
I confess, this the best I've ever had,
All in my feelings, I ain't mad, Pullout Game.

Didn't cover up before jumping in,
Barefooted, knock-kneed, inhaler right beside me.
Muscles palpitating blood through my main vein,
I'm trying not to scream her name, Pullout Game.

Section 1: Life

Legs getting heavy with all this biscuit and gravy,
Slipping in and out, trying to bow out gracefully.
Salt and precipitation impact my peripheral vision,
So hard to stop,
Is this all worth my name,
Pleasure, fame, naw it's My Pullout Game.

Dog Ears

Scoping and staying low-key,
Incognito is how I breathe.
Posted in my smoked-out Bentley,
Old school with hood credibility.

Ears to the streets, you know what it do,
Slowly passing through with nothing to prove.
Plotting and strategizing deep in the night,
Close to my enemies in case they take flight.

Paranoid from all this dope dealing,
Shipment from the basement to the ceiling.
Heat in my waist, to protect my place,
Not tryna catch another case.

Ain't going back to the penitentiary,
Just trying to stay sucka-free.
They still tryna bring me down,
So they can lock me up downtown.

I'm trying to change from my crooked ways.
I want to live and see another day.
I still gotta feed my seeds,
And take care of my responsibilities.

Yes I'm stubborn and set in my ways,
I'm a street dude and used to getting paid.
I ain't tryna hear what anybody say,
If I'm caught slipping may not live another day.

Section 1: Life

Don't know how to change or where to start.
I'm tired of trusting people with my heart.
Been burnt too many times,
With folks tryna sabotage my mind.

I'm a rider and refuse to give in,
I fight for mine until the end.
I got more enemies than friends,
Will this old dog ever trust again?

War Within

The WAR inside my mind and heart will end so I can live AGAIN..
My LIFE will not be bound by bad choices, failures and continuous DISTRACTIONS...
I will fight with the SWORD of the spirit activating God's weaponry on all demonic forces that want me to FAIL..........
My PRAYER LIFE will lead to better life choices and decisions regardless of the promises of MAN.........
FAMILY and FRIENDS will no longer influence me to see things their way if it doesn't align with God's WORD.........
My PRIDE and ARROGANCE will no longer keep me from receiving all that God has for my LIFE.........
GUILT will no longer impact my consciousness and block me from being prosperous and FRUITFUL.........
By FORGIVING, I will experience healthy and successful RELATIONSHIPS..........
My PAIN and SUFFERING will no longer block my healing process, because I want another chance to TRUST and LOVE AGAIN..........
I will not WORRY about things that are out of my control, but will do better managing my ANXIETY, STRESS and HEALTH..........
With God as the HEAD in my life, I will win the WAR WITHIN..........

SECTION 2

LESSONS

Waiting May Endure

Life is not my number one fan.
Why is medicine in high demand.
How much pain can I take.
If I crash, will this be my fate.

My feelings weigh so heavily.
My body is filled with anxiety.
My face wears a somber frown.
My tears keep pouring down.

I'm stuck like cemented bubble gum.
Sweat dripping heavily from the sun.
Impatience burns through my pancreas.
Feeling disabled asking God what's next.

My faith is shaky and I'm barely getting through.
Why does my attitude lack the proper fortitude.
Does my suffering have an expiration.
Do I continue or submit my resignation.

Trying hard not to overthink.
Sometimes I feel like the weakest link.
Prayer doesn't feel like it's working.
Hope is failing and my heart is still hurting.

Oh Lord, teach me how to wait on you.
Remove all distractions and change my attitude.
I wait patiently for your instructions above.
I humbly submit to your undying love.

NO Power

Saying yes is turning into stress.
Why should my best be any less.
Killing myself is nonsense.
How long should I straddle the fence?

I bend over backwards for you,
I truly question your aptitude.
This doesn't make any sense.
Why is every conversation so intense.

From date night to weekend getaways,
You always have something negative to say.
I believe arguing is your first love,
Getting mad raises your temperature up.

You always have a negative attitude,
Why do you pout when it's not about you.
Whenever in need I'm there consistently,
When it comes to me you run freely.

This has been going on for weeks,
I express my needs, you turn the other cheek.
I cater to you with plenty of joy,
You grudgingly give and stay annoyed.

Saying yes is giving me stress…
Saying yes is exhausting at best…
Saying yes gives you security…
Saying yes questions my durability…

Section 2: Lessons

The tables are now turning,
Learning to say NO is what I'm discerning.
I'm setting boundaries from now on,
If you can't accept my NO, you have to go.

I will not be mistreated and abused,
I will not be manipulated and used.
I will not be disregarded and denied,
When I say NO, respect my why.

Fake Grass

God has forgiven every sin,
God reveals everything within.
God can stop a car crash,
God can cough up cash.

Life isn't all that it's cracked up to be,
Life will have you hanging from a tree.
Life will vomit everything you said,
Life will awaken anything dead.

People will come and go,
People will lie and sell their souls.
People will steal your name,
People will play foolish games.

Never thought life could be unfair,
Never thought life would play truth or dare.
Never knew pretentious people truly exist,
Never knew friends would make that list.

My heart is deceived by pain,
My heart feels so estranged.
My heart doesn't trust anymore,
My heart level is borderline poor.

Love is supposed to be real,
Love is supposed to express and feel.
Love is supposed to be fair and true,
Love is supposed to stay fresh and new.

Section 2: Lessons

Grass stays green when watered and manicured,
Grass stays healthy with fertilizer and manure.
Grass absorbs light energy from the sun through chlorophyll,
Grass can stay green if it's God's will.

Break My Fall

Lord, cover me when I fall,
Give me strength to stand tall.
Laser my eyes to see clearly,
Releasing all bondage and iniquity.

Guilt occupies my mind,
Pain continues to be unkind.
If waiting is your divine strategy,
Open my heart and minister to me.

Do I stand still and wait for your call?
Do I continue building my prayer wall?
Are you shaping my character and faith?
Is your patience teaching me how to wait?

I lean on you to avoid bad choices,
I pray fervently to block out voices.
I continue walking in power and strength,
Seeking you with both knees bent.

I can't escape this spiritual warfare,
All of these attacks are so unfair.
I continue fighting with undying faith,
God promises He will never forsake.

God is who I believe in,
He washes away every sin.
He honors repentance and confession,
With every fall there is a lesson.

Love My Hate

Hate and love got my hands tied.
Mercy sneaks up from the backside.
My heart can't mask this subtle jab.
My self-control is not going to last.

My mind is losing time,
Thoughts continue pressing rewind.
Holding on to promises kept,
Trusting God with nothing left.

Scanning the inner man for clues.
My tank is running out of fuel.
Trying to maintain the right attitude.
And not respond the way I want to.

My love and hate continues to recalibrate,
It's not about who lost or won,
But understanding why God sacrificed His son.
And forgiving those for what they have done.

I hate that love got me feeling this way,
Praying that my heart won't go astray.
I'm trying to love with the Potters heart,
Trying to depart from all wicked thoughts.

God shines His light in clear view,
Showing me what I'm commissioned to do.
I know darkness cannot survive in light,
So I must flood love every day and night.

Ricky Lamon Davis

If hate knew how to love, like love does hate,
Then love can teach hate before it's too late.
Hate has a chance to put the axe down,
Before it's too late and the trumpet sounds.

Ignorantly Blind

Eyeballs and sockets were interwoven,
When God created man and woman.
There's no illusion to this phenomenon,
Nor the trajectory of where we came from.

Lies continue to separate from the truth,
Society chooses what to dispute.
Manipulation creates deception in disguise,
Leading anyone to a sacrificial demise.

Will I escape this mind state of rape?
Do I hesitate, calculate, or wait?
Challenge what I see with integrity?
Or fall victim to the devil's plot to kill me?

God's word addresses every issue in life,
From trust, faith, prayer, belief and sacrifice.
Interpretation is critical to receive authentic proclamation,
Hebrew, Greek and Aramaic speak clear revelation.

The truth is sometimes altered by pulpit pimps,
Some try to change what's already in print.
Persuading the mind to adapt to present time,
With more focus on self, prosperity and wealth.

My eyes are built to see the glory,
My tears and fears cry a different story.
My conscience tells my heart what's right,
My mind and soul continue to fight.

Ricky Lamon Davis

How do I show myself approved...
How do I defend God's way in school...
How do I act when verbally attacked...
How do I counter biblical facts...

Since God allows me to see..
I don't have to think ignorantly..
I can walk by faith and not by sight,
Rest on truth and defend what's right.

Artificiality

Dazed in amazement by her beauty,
Looked at me and said hello cutie.
Smitten by her eyes and glossy lips,
Blew kisses through her painted fingertips.

Her eyes would cause an insomniac to dream,
Her hour shaped curves swiveled freely.
Her beautiful body had me feeling naughty,
Still can't believe what's in front of me.

Butterfly lashes dripped in high fashion,
Honey blonde streaks matched her cheeks.
Make-up layered and so much hair,
Hard to tell if she had a BBL.

In my eyes she was better than AI,
I didn't care if she was fake or real.
Loved her voice and physical touch,
Captivated me enough to miss lunch.

Her image was hypnotizing and relaxing,
I knew it was temporary satisfaction.
But her magnetism jolted another reaction,
Causing my DNA to sprang into action.

Shocked and dismayed, been up for days,
Bloodshot eyes made nightfall feel like sunrise,
Realized virtual reality ain't for me,
I need a real woman, not some Artificiality.

Tailor Made

Is inner beauty hard to find,
Is an SOS signal ever on time?
Are dating sites truly legit?
Are people really getting catfished?

My lady is already made,
God created her on the 6th day.
Out of 24, He only used one,
Grabbed his rib and created a woman.

She's already here, ready and pure,
Just have to be patient and catch up to her.
I imagine my woman to be beautifully intelligent,
God-fearing, loving, unselfish and diligent.

I want to know what brings her peace,
How big is her heart and will I need a key.
Is fellowship with God a priority,
Is she a kingdom builder or recruiter for her sorority?

Does she practice controlling her emotions?
Does she start her mornings with daily devotions?
Will she nurture and love unconditionally?
Will we grow spiritually and emotionally?

Helpmates pray and cry together,
Intentionally making the relationship better.
Storms will come and the snow will thicken,
The devil will use anything to creep in.

Section 2: Lessons

Maturity is necessary no time for games,
Loving each other consistently will help ease the pain.
I need compromising and effective communication,
Someone who's not demanding but understanding.

God made woman as the life-bringer and giver.
God made her to nourish, nurture, feed, and console.
No need to be anxious, I will stand and wait,
To finally meet my tailor-made soulmate.

Blood Water

This mirror image reflects we.
God's likeness is a reflection of me.
Not just the cacao olive skin.
Or kinky hair fighting the wind.

Past generations left unanswered scars.
Tribes ruled slaves and families migrated far. Does heritage and culture define who we are.
Which race continues to make life hard.

This bloodline is not mine,
It's mixed with so many kinds.
Prayer is necessary for all color lines,
Racism makes love hard to find.

Families fight and won't defend what's right.
Someone dies and real estate goes to probate.
Why can't the foolishness and drama cease?
Why can't Big Momma Rest in Peace?

Is blood really thicker than water?
Is the Matriarch the oldest daughter?
Is jealousy a thorn between siblings?
Why pretend every Thanksgiving?

No one talks about Daddy's secret love child,
And the extra family he hid for a while.
Can't hide the incestuous acts on Momma's side,
Along with sexual abuse and addictive alcohol use.

Section 2: Lessons

Family strife cuts deeper than hibachi knives.
Why are family secrets destroying innocent lives?
How does a family heal from brokenness?
Will we ever reverse this generational curse?

Family hurt can't be ignored.
How much pain can our families afford?
Can God still prune the family tree?
Why did God allow slavery?

If we return to plowing and sowing,
God will cut all branches not growing.
By laying our troubles at the altar and learning to trust more,
Our prayers will make families stronger than before.

Grand of Things

Recognized for her fame in God's name.
Saved, sanctified, and filled with the holy ghost, feared, envied, hated, and resented by most.
Traveled and lived far and wide from the south, west, and the East Coast.

Her name was Earnestine, a woman who loved to sing,
Plant okra, tomatoes, green onions, bell peppers, and collard greens.
Her thumb was green by nature, growing plants was her specialty,
She loved the outdoors and enjoyed fishing by the sea.

We knew her as Grandma, a lady who threw down in the kitchen,
Cooking hot water cornbread, pinto beans, rice, gravy, and smothered chicken.
Not to mention her words of wisdom and the things she said at times,
Get right or go left, it's tight but it's right and a hard head totes a sore behind.

We knew her as Mom, a wise vessel who discerned anything from heaven to hell, lecturing, preaching, braiding her own hair and cracking pecans out the shell.
Singing this little light of mine, I'm gonna let it shine about 50 million times,
A song that kept her smiling when things weren't always fine.

Section 2: Lessons

We knew her as Evangelist, a vessel of God, ministering to the young and old,
Touching many lives, praying to save souls.
Her passion for Christ was contagious, spreading the gospel in Jesus name,
Job well done as we celebrate this vessel of God in the Grand of Things.

SECTION 3

LOVE

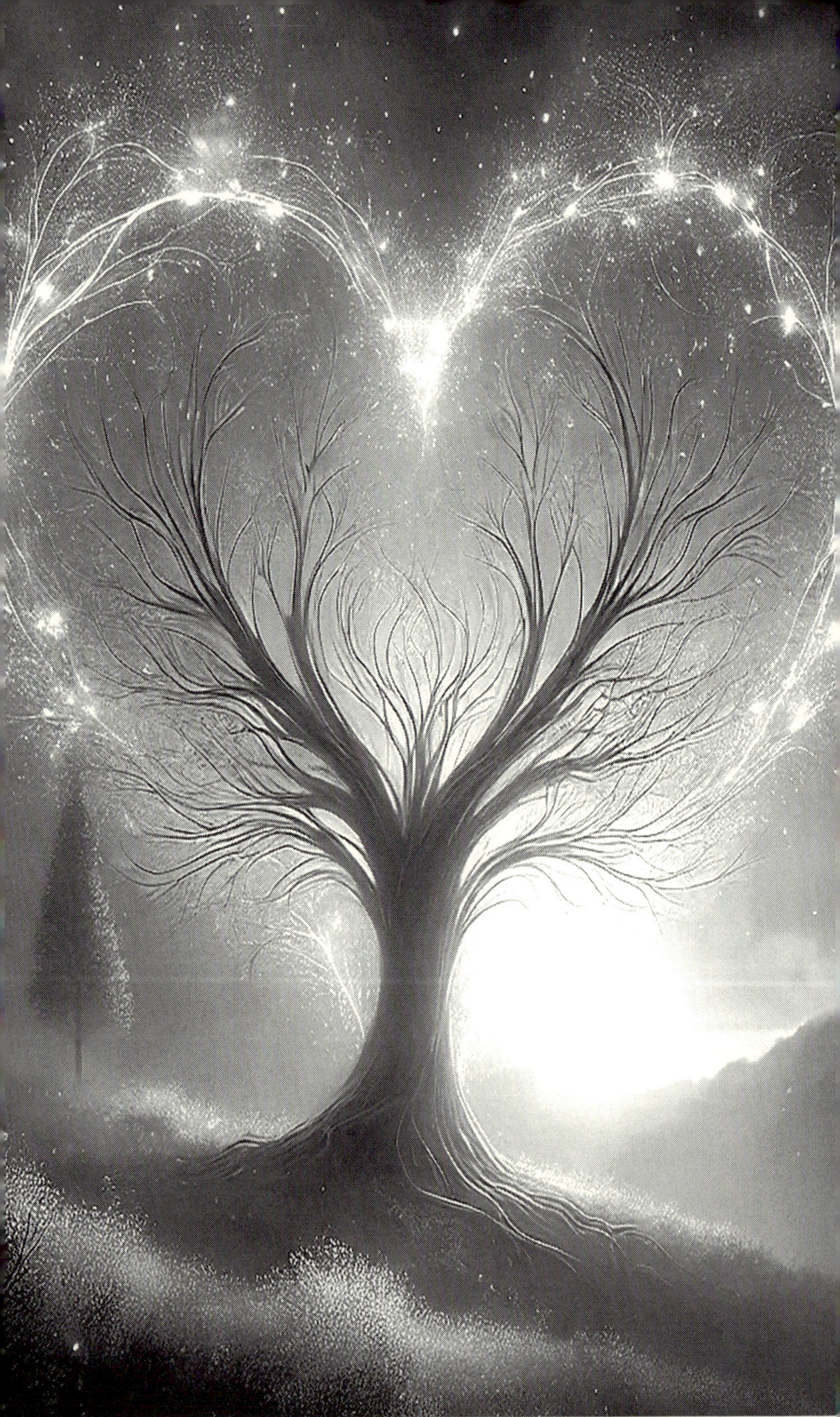

LuvFriend

Angels fly to the beat of God's heart,
The way you do mine when we're apart.
Your voice synthesizes a thousand violins,
Creating rich, beautiful melodies from within.

No matter the distance between us,
Our luv has a special kind of trust.
No matter the fear you once had,
I luv making you smile when you're sad.

Luv can wait until our next date,
Luv can wait and won't be late.
Luv can wait and make sweet memories,
Luv can wait and bring you close to me.

Friends will come and go,
Friends won't support every show.
Friends will flake without warning,
Friends will disappear when it's storming.

My petition to you will never change,
My friendship with you remains the same.
My luv continues to chase your name,
My heart beats fast like a locomotive train.

Time will reveal if this luv's for real,
Time will heal any pain you feel.
Time will cast out all doubts and fears,
Time will allow space for you to shed tears.

Ricky Lamon Davis

Take this time and examine your heart, Reflect on us when we're apart.
Take plenty of time and heal from your past,
When that's done, prepare for what you have.

Still Love

Today I propose a toast,
To a woman I love the most.
Whose spirit is warm and tender,
And beautiful as autumn in November.

She's more patient than I've ever seen.
Days I'm exhausted and running out of steam.
She talks less and allows me to decompress.
Quietly telling me to get some rest.

She provides comfort underneath my skin,
Gently rubbing my head and caressing my chin.
She keeps me anchored in her lake of love,
What more can a man dream of.

When she listens it keeps me calm and still,
Making me vulnerable in how I feel.
Without confrontation or emasculation,
Her respect for me is the perfect combination.

She fills me up with her love to drink,
She challenges my mind and causes me to think.
She's the calm to my storm and won't let me drown,
She labors in the kitchen without a frown.

She's mastered the art of spoiling my heart.
Eucalyptus baths and massages after dark.
If I'm sick she makes me better.
Nurturing me no matter the weather.

Date nights she loves driving my car,
Taking long rides under shooting stars. Praying and affirming me every day,
Believing and covering me in faith.

She is more than icing on the cake,
She was definitely worth the wait.
I'm grateful for the blessings above,
I'm perfectly satisfied with this kind of love.

Matching Luggage

Do you date with intentions?
Do you enjoy intimacy and kissing?
What are your long-term goals?
I'm interested to see where this goes.

Let's take inventory before we continue.
Is there anything hidden on the menu?
Are we exclusive or am I sharing you?
Is this a thing or you want a ring by spring?

When together we have much in common,
Is this serious or you got something else poppin'?
Just tell me because my time is valuable,
If this road ends we can just be friends.

Before taking this journey, we have to match.
Our connection needs to endure any rough patch.
Are we emotionally mature to handle each other,
Do you consider yourself an unselfish lover?

Any past abuse we need to discuss?
Are there any trust issues between us?
Are you willing to be transparent and vulnerable,
Do you relax at home or love being on the go?

What's your take on the ecosystem and politics?
Do you exercise, eat healthy and take vitamin supplements?
How long do you sleep and what's your morning routine?
Are you domesticated and enjoy keeping a house clean?

Ricky Lamon Davis

Mental stability is important to me,
Do you believe in therapy, self-care and theology?
I enjoy family time and fellowshipping with friends,
I'm a follower of Christ and not secular trends.

I enjoy cooking, sports and watching movies,
I enjoy wine, mixed drinks, H2O, and smoothies.
I enjoy swimming, Jacuzzis and bubble baths,
I enjoy entertainment, music, and a good laugh.

I understand your desire for settling down,
I'm all about action and not how something sounds.
I desire a lifelong commitment with full health coverage,
Let's continue and see if we have matching luggage.

Daddy Man

Uncomfortable as it may seem,
Real fathers carry huge responsibilities.
Baby daddies are different than daddy men,
When it comes to kids, real men don't pretend.

It's time to turn a new leaf,
Control your anger and squash the beef.
Seize the opportunity and correct your wrongs,
Change your tune and produce new songs.

History repeated keeps you defeated.
Forgiving your past heals the heart fast.
How long will this generational curse last?
Ask God how to navigate your present task.

Kids are rejected and daddies keep neglecting,
Without parenting what examples are you setting?
It's okay if you don't know everything, Reach out
to fathers who still in the game.

Daddies should practice what they preach,
Investing time in every lesson they teach.
Displaying more patience and less frustration,
Boosting self-esteem, self-awareness and motivation.

Mad at your kids for calling their step-father dad.
Why punish them because you feel bad?
Don't be sad just spend more time,
Move forward and leave the past behind.

They can't take your Fathers day away.
They won't hate you if you stay.
They will substitute you if you're absent.
They can't force you to be present.

Your responsibility was God-giving,
The moment that embryo started living.
You had 9 months to develop a plan,
So what's the problem, man?

Full-time daddies are a rare commodity,
Fathers are designed to raise little somebodies.
To be strong, healthy, courageous, and confident,
To teach, cover, protect, and nurture what God sent.

Teach your little girl how to date,
The truth about sex and why she must wait.
Teach your boy about the birds and bees,
How to cherish and respect every girl he meets.

Mothers can't turn boys into men,
Mothers struggle being their sons' disciplinarian.
Mothers shouldn't have to give their daughters away,
Mothers shouldn't be their daughters' first date.

It takes a willing man to be a daddy,
The same way a golfer needs a caddy.
Kids need fathers who are on demand,
So stand up and be a real daddy, man.

Couch Talk

Something is telling me to pull over,
I burst out crying in the Range Rover.
With so many continuous tears,
I'm now confronted with my worst fears.

Mind is racing and my heart beats fast,
Body is weakening and running out of gas.
Can't stop the numbness in my feet,
Tongue is swollen and can hardly speak.

I feel anxious, stressed, and full of sweat,
I'm scared, nervous and my clothes are soaking wet.
With degrees and licenses, I am not a dummy,
I have a great job, family, and plenty of money.

I'm on the cuff of a nervous breakdown,
I want to disappear and never be found.
I barely eat and dropping serious weight,
I frequent happy hour and stay out late.

What should I do, Doc? I'm losing control.
Had a fight with my neighbor, because of my anger.
Wifey is threatening to give back the ring I gave her.
Kids are scorned and won't talk to me anymore.

I can't lose my family, they're all I got,
How can I get this nonsense to stop?
I should invest more in family and less in stocks,
Be accessible and not work around the clock.

Ricky Lamon Davis

It's hard being accountable,
Getting blamed and letting things go.
How do I fight for something I've never had,
When I never received affection from my own dad?

How do I process past hurt?
Is my heart qualified to show its worth?
Where is the line drawn from right and wrong,
What is the time limit and for how long?

Why so much patience in dealing with me,
Your questions help me think logically.
Thanks for listening and allowing me to unload,
It's almost ninety minutes, where did the time go?

You sure this therapy thing ain't no scam,
It's hard opening up and sharing who I am.
It feels good expressing myself and not be judged,
I will commit to therapy, if nothing else to work on myself.

Fluent Love

I realize your interest in me,
And surprised by what I see.
Is my personality stimulating to you.
I'm interested, so let's get to it.

What's your career, are you in school?
How do you feel meeting someone new?
Are you open to new possibilities?
Name some of your God-given abilities.

Are you receptive to a variety of lessons?
 Do you intentionally keep people guessing?
Do you like a challenge or the easy route?
Are you a giver, taker, or heartbreaker?

I appreciate uplifting conversations.
Feeding my mind with stimulating dilation.
Satisfying me doesn't take much.
Consistency is what fills my cup.

I carry myself like I've already won.
Head raised high to receive the morning sun.
If your light shines, it will match mine.
Then God will reveal His heavenly sign.

I'm fluent in all 5 love languages.
I've traveled far to study the heart.
Searching and exploring to get understanding.
Discovering what makes love so demanding.

Ricky Lamon Davis

Words of affirmation; let me encourage and listen to you.
Physical touch; I want to kiss, hug, and stay booed up.
Gifts; I will give and demonstrate what you appreciate.
Quality time; when it's date night, phones off, you're all mine.
Acts of service; I will cook, clean, and massage everything.

If a locksmith specializes in security devices and locks,
And a mechanic services engines, brakes, and car shocks,
If a robotics scientist designs, builds and tests robots,
It can't be hard to love someone's heart until it stops.

I am well-rounded, adaptable and flexible.
I am tender, kind, loving, romantic and sensual.
I can be best friend, homey lover, and ride to die.
I can be a skywriter and message you from the sky.

If you want to travel this journey with me,
We must serve the same God equally.
Can we walk and agree spiritually?
Are you capable of loving me unconditionally?

I Will Find You

All naturally dipped in vitamin E,
Online dating ain't for me.
No red flags or men in drag,
Is why my patience is at level 3.

Not in the red-light district.
Not at the tattoo expo.
Not at the fashion show.
Not at the end of cupid's bow.

How far should I look?
At a park reading a book,
A restaurant as the head cook,
Or a desolate, cozy, hidden nook?

One of my biggest dreams,
Is to find a good thing.
I'm ready to celebrate, laugh, and sing,
Too old to settle for any fling.

I patiently await alone and free,
For a woman made just for me.
Friends with benefits and situationships,
Is not enough for a meaningful relationship.

I've traveled, searched and veered wide,
Made wrong turns and ignored yield signs.
I now receive the voice of Elohim,
As he gives instructions in my dreams.

Ricky Lamon Davis

My capacity continues to overflow,
My faith in Abba Father continues to grow.
My spiritual man is glowing.
My trust in God is flowing.

So if I attend night watch service,
Or even corporate prayer,
Maybe at Sunday worship,
Wherever it is, I will find her there.

Music Me

Come bring me your sweetness,
I want to know what love is.
If only for one night,
Everything is going to be alright.

Stop, look, listen to your heart,
So be very careful not to let us part.
Hey, love, turn your head around,
Girl, you make my love come down.

You're as right as rain,
It's a thin line between love and hate.
You're a big girl now, no more daddy's little girl,
Only if I gave you diamonds and pearls.

Never be, be a better love,
We can make it if we try, just the two of us.
The closer I get to you,
Girl, I'm hooked on you, nothing else I'd rather do.

Strolling in the park, watching winter turn to spring,
I hope your image of me is what I hope to be,
You are my starship come take me out tonight,
If loving you is wrong, I don't want to be right.

If this world were mine, I will place at your feet,
I crossed the wildest sea nothin' could discourage me.
You're my darlin', darlin' baby,
The smell of her just drives me crazy.

Ricky Lamon Davis

Loving you is like a dream come true,
You own my heart and mind, I truly adore you.
What we have is much more than they can see,
'Cause you mean the world to me, you are my everything.

Oh, last night, me and my woman; we cried together,
Loving you whether, whether times are good or bad, happy or sad.
Every day, love me in your own special way,
No matter how long it takes, I've got time, baby, I'll wait.

Quantum Covenant

My future wife, I must confess,
My happy heart needs to be addressed.
Prayers have been answered, and I'm convinced,
Waiting on the Lord makes perfect sense.

My petition to God was very specific,
No science, philosophy, or quantum physics.
A leap of faith required submission,
For God to navigate my search engine.

A relational woman putting God before me,
A virtuous woman who casts her burdens freely.
A woman who believes in prayer over politics,
A woman who purposely embraces her spiritual gifts.

I've learned to listen more than speak,
And pay close attention to her speech.
Hoping her words and actions are the same,
Before proposing and extending my name.

I learned early in discipleship class,
What makes a covenant marriage last?
It's God's binding, covering between husband and wife,
And submitting to a divine understanding for life.

As God leads the relationship, His plan is suffice,
His directions are clear, effective, and precise.
He challenges us daily to test our faith,
To see if we have the patience to wait.

It takes a quantum leap of faith,
To enter a union with a soulmate.
It takes a covenant marriage,
For God to bless a union and carriage.

Flashy weddings never outlast engagement festivities,
Imagery and validation shows how the union will be.
Superficial and selfish behaviors ruin friends and families,
In the name of, "It's all about me."

Will you marry for love or living good?
Will you marry for God or Hollywood?
Will you marry for longevity or prosperity.
Or marry for a Quantum Covenant and integrity?

Love Is

Before Jumping the Broom,
It needs to be Just Wright and good.
To have unlimited Brown Sugar,
Love and Basketball in the Wood.

Does love fall from trees?
Does love sting like bees?
Is love a censor detector?
Is love its own protector?

Love covers a multitude of sins.
Love pumps blood until the end.
Love can forgive a murderer.
Love can show mercy to a burglar.

Love is patient and kind.
Love respects the process of time.
Love is unselfish and giving.
Love never fails when you're living.

I desire agape love like no other.
That selfless, unconditional love like my mother.
I want Eros' love to demonstrate satisfaction.
That romantic love and physical attraction.

I want Phileo love to treat me fairly.
Loving my brothers, friends, and family.
I want Pragma love to feed my soul.
A love that's compatible, committed, and practical.

Ricky Lamon Davis

Love is God and God is Love.
And God defines what true Love is.
Love isn't Love without the Creator above.
So if Love is Love, then God can't be in it.

About the Author

Ricky Lamon Davis is a motivational speaker, public speaker, leadership and community development trainer, health and wellness expert, podcast host, and author.

Made in the USA
Columbia, SC
02 June 2025